23 Ways to Jump Start Your Human Resources Career

Diane M. Pfadenhauer, SPHR, Esq.

www.hrcareerjumpstart.com

23 Ways to Jump Start Your Human Resources Career

Diane M. Pfadenhauer, SPHR, Esq.

DataMotion Publishing, LLC

New York

23 Ways to Jump Start Your Human Resources Career

ISBN: 978-1-937299-00-2 (paperback)

ISBN: 978-1-937299-01-9 (ePub)

DataMotion Publishing, LLC
1019 Fort Salonga Road, Suite 10-333
Northport, NY 11768-2209
www.datamotionpublishing.com

Table of Contents

∿∿∿∿∿∿∿∿∿

About the Author

Diane M. Pfadenhauer, SPHR, Esq.

With over 25 years of experience in human resources and as an attorney, Diane is president of Employment Practices Advisors, Inc., a boutique firm specializing in employment litigation consulting (including workplace investigations and expert witness testimony on human resource practices) and human resource consulting encompassing a broad spectrum of tactical and strategic human resource practices. For the past 10 years she has been a professor in the M.B.A. program at St. Joseph's College in New York. Prior to her position at St. Joseph's, she spent over a decade as an adjunct professor in graduate programs throughout the New York metropolitan area.

An active member in community and professional organizations, Diane is admitted to the New York State Bar. As a member of the National Speaker's Association, she is a frequent speaker and writer and her articles have appeared in industry publications including *HR Magazine, HR Advisor, the Journal of Private Equity, Law Technology News, the Journal of Corporate Renewal,* and the New York Bar Association. She is certified as a Senior Professional in Human Resources (SPHR) by the Human Resources Certification Institute.

Diane is also the writer of the award winning weblog, www.strategichrlawyer.com, read by over 25,000 unique visitors per month from over 50 countries, as well as the author of several books on the subjects of human resources and employment law. She was recently awarded the *New York State*

Liberty Award for her Pro Bono work in Louisiana following the devastation of Hurricane Katrina.

Diane received her law degree, *cum laude*, from St. John's University School of Law where she was awarded the ABA/BNA Award for Excellence in the Study of Labor and Employment Law. She is a graduate of New York Institute of Technology's Center for Labor and Industrial Relations where she received her M.S., with *distinction*. She received her B.A. from S.U.N.Y. Potsdam, majoring in Industrial Labor Relations.

Warning-Disclaimer

While this book strives to provide the reader with practical guidance and to provide general education on the topic at hand, it is not a substitute for adequate legal or other professional advice. The opinions within represent the opinions of the authors and editors only and, therefore, should not be construed as a position on the part of any particular organization or entity.

Further, nothing herein should be construed as the rendering of legal or other professional advice and the reader is advised to consult with appropriate counsel for obtaining any advice or acting upon any of the information contained herein. By reading this publication, no attorney client relationship exists between the reader and either the author or publisher.

ᴎᴎᴎᴎᴎᴎᴎᴎ

Introduction

re you in a professional rut? Feeling unappreciated? Lost your HR mojo? Starting to hate your career? Willing to work at a convenience store just to get away from human resources?

I spent over 20 years in human resources becoming a lawyer along the way. I started out six feet tall and now am barely five feet two inches tall. I've learned first-hand how to completely mess up a human resources department and how to make one respected.

Every division of the company thinks that it is the subject of bashing or disrespect by others, and the human resources department is certainly not alone in this regard. The legal department thinks that no one listens to its advice. The marketing department thinks that everyone believes they can do their job. In human resources, however, there are several constituents that judge us – employees, managers, the community and the company overall.

The human resources profession is about credibility. Everything you do hinges upon how you are perceived – sometimes more often than how well you do your job. The good news is that YOU can positively influence your perception among your constituents. And, you can start this change TODAY!

This guide is intended to provide you with guidance and specific tools that you can begin using TODAY to improve your reputation, increase your credibility, move ahead in your career and gain the respect you believe you deserve. Yes, you may have heard of some of these before. But, it's time to dust off those cobwebs, give yourself a pat on the back, remember

why you chose this profession, feel good about yourself because you made a difference, and wake up with a smile. Let
this little guide serve as a way to remind you to change even
just one thing. Did I mention that you can start today?

What are you waiting for?

∿∿∿∿∿∿∿∿∿∿

1. Don't Plan the Company Picnic or Holiday Party, Ever

*I*f you are doing this now, delegate to someone else. When I was a senior human resources leader, one of my first goals was to get my department out of the party planning business. You will never be respected as a business leader unless you do.

In the eyes of your co-workers, anyone can plan a party. It will take too much of your time – time that you should be spending doing real work, learning something productive or solving a worthwhile problem. In addition, you do not want to be associated with complaints regarding restaurant food, poor catering or after parties.

So, how do you get out of this mess?

- Delegate to someone in your department and distance yourself from it.
- Form a committee of employees from around the company that can plan the party – then run... quickly.
- If you have never had a company holiday party or picnic and someone asks you to plan one, say no!

ᴎᴎᴎᴎᴎᴎᴎᴎᴎ

2. Don't Ever Manage Facilities, Security or the Front Desk

Just because you are an expert in managing people, that does not make you an expert in managing security or facilities. Unfortunately, however, many human resources professionals gravitate toward the thrill of taking on more responsibility (probably under the guise of feeling like they are appreciated or being duped into a false promotion) by taking on the job that most other people don't want. Seriously, do you think anyone else in their right mind in your organization would be crazy enough to voluntarily deal with bathroom issues, complaints about the heat or air conditioning, whether someone brought in their identification card today, etc? Not on your life. They usually explain that they are too busy doing real work – this could include making money for the company, solving business problems, and the like.

Worse than facilities and security is managing the front desk. This thrusts the human resources professional into a world of insanity – scheduling the answering of phones, managing the receptionist and, worse yet, when the receptionist is out sick, guess who ends up answering the phone? Someone in human resources.

So now that the human resources professional has taken on this new responsibility, guess who gets all of the nonsensical questions? You guessed it. I once heard of a regional human resources manager who received a complaint from another manager about the fact that the toilet paper in the rest room did not rip on the perforation. Two college degrees, advanced certification and twenty years of experience led to this kind of existence!

So how do you get out of this mess?

- Give it to the CFO. He or she is likely controlling the budget anyway. And when the toilet paper does not rip on the perforation, he or she can increase the budget to buy better toilet paper.
- Delegate to someone in your department and let them manage it. Address only those things that are critical to corporate security, significant issues of safety and the like.
- Hire professionals. If you have to be tasked with these responsibilities, manage them professionally.

NNNNNNNNN

3. Don't Rely on "the Law" as the Source of Your Power

One of the biggest things that human resources professionals rely upon as a source of power is touting the law. The law gives you power. The law makes you look smart. If you tell your managers that they cannot do something because it's illegal, they actually listen to you.

On the other hand, if you tell them not to do something because it just makes sense, you are ignored. So what do human resources practitioners do? Cite the law as the basis for all of their decisions and communicate in that manner.

I once knew a human resources manager who cited her outside labor and employment counsel continuously, all the time, to the point where it was nauseating. She forgot, however, several important concepts. First, lawyers give advice on the law. Business people run businesses. This means that lawyers don't actually tell you what to do. Your job is to interpret what they say and apply it in your business. Second, most of the time when a lawyer tells a human resources person something it is a recommendation. Companies ignore lawyers all the time. Trust me; I know this. Lastly, using lawyers in this fashion gets really expensive. If the human resources professional is calling the lawyer to figure out how to run human resources, that's a problem.

What the human resources manager in the above example failed to realize is that she did absolutely nothing to help her credibility. In fact, she made herself look incompetent. She could not convince someone to do something because it was right, ethical correct, reasonable, or based on good judgment. Eventually, everyone ignored her and gave up asking her anything.

The problem here becomes even further compounded because once the human resources professional falls into this trap, the constituents begin to question his/her answers. All it takes is one person who knows more about the law than the human resources professional or for the human resources professional to answer incorrectly or mislead someone and he/she will never be believed or trusted again. The biggest insult usually occurs when the human resources professional touts the law to someone at the senior level of the organization who gives up and calls the lawyer himself/herself.

What the human resources professional in this trap also does not realize is that in most instances he/she is not a lawyer and lacks any and all credibility giving legal advice.

So in conversation after conversation, the human resources professional says something is illegal or says that the lawyer made them do it. Eventually the constituents give up and either stop asking or just call the lawyer themselves.

So how do you get out of this mess?

- Become a lawyer. I did. But, it's really expensive.
- Focus on employee performance and solving real business and employee problems as your source of power.
- Use the law to educate managers and employees. It's not a secret area of knowledge that only you know about.

When you cite the law, cite the law first. Then, discuss with your fellow managers the possible solutions and outcomes to the problem. Your job is to make sure employees are treated in a manner that is fair and equitable. You can advocate for salvaging an employee or to fire an employee. Use judgment and facts in your arguments once everyone is clear what the law is. For the control freaks among us, this is often the hardest.

The human resources professional that touts the law is often using it as a way to control or as a crutch.

Trust me; you can do this!

NNNNNNNNN

4. Solve a Business Problem – Even a Small One

Human resources professionals are often referred to as "they." Usually when described in such a way, there is usually a finger pointing to "over there." This infers that human resources is somehow distinct and separate from management and employees. When this happens on the part of management, it usually stems from the perception or belief that human resources is not business. More specifically, from the belief that human resources cannot help managers solve a business problem they are facing.

Getting involved in business is always easier when you are the new kid on the block. When you are the new human resources professional, you just start getting involved with those nonbelievers who would have challenged you if you had been there for a while. They will give you the courtesy of getting involved in their business – at a minimum to see what you can come up with.

As the new human resources professional, if you are confronted with a manager who is not used to having human resources involved in the management of their business, start with something small that has people/employee implications. This may include:

- Modifying the staffing in the department in order to control overtime.
- Creating job descriptions where they didn't previously exist.
- Analyzing performance issues, before they come to human resources, which may indicate a training need.

The key is to use your expertise to solve THEIR problem. At this point "no" is not a word in your vocabulary.

As the human resources professional who has been around for a while, you need to make a paradigm shift. Assume the worst and start small.

- Take baby steps to get to know your managers.
- Start with a new manager who has joined your organization and make him/her your biggest fan.
- Start with an employee who has just been promoted to management and coach him/her along.
- Start with a manger you trust.

The key in all of this is to have little successes. These little successes will create fans throughout the organization. Little success will lead to bigger ones, and before you know it, you will be well entrenched in the business of the business solving big problems and making lots of money.

ᴎᴎᴎᴎᴎᴎᴎᴎᴎ

5. Learn Your Industry, Know Your Company's Competition, and Know How Your Company Makes Money

Most organizations sell a product, sell a service or receive funding for their operations. Your job is to understand how that money comes in, how it is spent, and how and/or when the organizations makes money. You know that you understand this when you can explain it, in detail, to someone else.

Is your industry contracting, growing or staying the same? Are your company's profits growing? Are your products competitive? How are your receivables, cash flow, and margins?

Human resources gurus talk about being business partners. You can only be a business partner if you understand business – deeply.

There are many sectors of the economy where experience in a particular industry is vital to being hired in senior levels of human resources. However, in many smaller organizations or at lower levels in the department, industry experience is not always a bar to being hired. The challenge, then, is to demonstrate your interest in learning about this new industry and how your role fits. Many human resources professionals, however, are afraid to ask any questions for fear of looking unknowledgeable or foolish. Little does one realize, however, that people like to talk about themselves.

In technology companies, it is not at all uncommon for the techno-geeks to look down upon the administrative staff because they understandably haven't a clue about the technology. The real success story comes when the human resources professional puts forth effort to learn and understand the technology.

How should you proceed, you ask?
- Read industry periodicals.
- Find a manager you can trust and ask them to teach you.
- Do external research.
- Learn how the organization makes money.
- Learn how the industry has evolved and where it is going.

- Ask your experts how you can contribute from a human resources perspective.
- Take a course.

NNNNNNNNNN

6. Attend a Staff Meeting - Not Your Own

One of the greatest compliments any human resources practitioner can receive is a request to attend a staff meeting of another department because the manager feels he/she is a valuable contributor and leader. Unfortunately, this does not always happen naturally. In fact, there will be those who will resist your presence. After all, you could be perceived as a spy or you "just don't belong" there.

Attending a staff meeting allows you to communicate at the business level with employees and managers who may have previously viewed you as completely uninvolved. It will also give you a perspective and understanding of the day to day challenges that the particular department faces. Lastly, it will allow you to learn about how the business operates from a broad perspective and how this particular department fits into the big picture. Find a manager you know and trust to let you sit in on one of their meetings.

At your first staffing meeting, be quiet. Just listen. Let the attendees get used to seeing you around. After all, you were the one that used to plan the company picnic. They are not used to having you involved in their day to day management or doing real work. Do not insult them on their turf by telling them how to do their jobs.

Plan in advance to redirect the meeting if it turns to focusing on human resources issues. Remember, you are trying to get away from a human resources session; begin to create an awareness and perception of you focusing on business.

You will be amazed at how your understanding of the department and its operations will positively influence your ability to find solutions to their problems. Show a real genuine interest and the rewards will come in spades!

NNNNNNNNN

7. Know Your Numbers

Measure something! OK, not anything. Measure something that matters even if in the most rudimentary way. You do not need fancy formulas, spread sheets or calculations. Focus in your area on an expense, a utilization, a loss, etc., and find a way to improve it. If it must be something associated with the company picnic, so be it.

What you do not want to do is measure something for the sake of measuring and ultimately demonstrate no value for your efforts. In my human resources life I would periodically stop sending reports of statistics we generated to see if anyone missed them. In most instances no one did.

Occasionally, I also found myself asking human resources professionals what they measure. They would respond with pretty spreadsheets showing turnover numbers or similar statistics. Then I asked them two questions. First, what do you do with these fancy spreadsheets? The usual response was that they were given to someone else. Then, I asked them what they learn and apply from them. That was usually the question that resulted in a blank stare.

I would often ask human resources departments if they were good at what they did. They most invariably answered with a resounding "yes." When I then asked them how they knew, the blank stares returned.

What to measure, you ask? It all starts with your business and how your role and department fit into it. What statistics matter in your organization? What statistics matter to the performance of your department? I can't tell you that all of these things are important in your organization or department, but they might be. Only you can decide and only you can determine what these measurements tell you. Here are just a few:

- Cost per hire
- Time it takes for human resources to screen and forward a qualified job candidate to a department
- Turnover (in some meaningful way)
- The extent to which certain benefits you offer are valued in your organization and by whom
- Retention – who stays and who goes and why.

∾∾∾∾∾∾∾∾∾

8. Act Like a Consultant

When I became a consultant I learned several things. First, if I didn't work, I didn't get paid. At work, I got paid whether I worked or not. Second, consultants are hired to solve problems and employees are hired to do work. But, consultants are generally paid more than employees. What does that tell you? Lastly, clients called me because they had real problems that needed solutions. Even if you are an employee, you must act like a consultant.

Have you ever noticed how consultants work? They come in, talk a lot, pontificate, delegate to employees and send a big bill. The key is the pontification. Here's what they do:

- They establish themselves as an expert.
- They garner trust.
- They recognize who pays them.
- They challenge the status quo respectfully.
- They listen.
- They learn about the organization.
- They recommend a solution to a real problem.
- They assist in implementing the solution.

Act like a consultant!

9. Don't Insist on Treating Everyone the Same

It should come as no surprise that I teach employment law. Every so often someone articulates rather assertively that organizations have to treat all employees equally. No, organizations do not have to treat all employees equally. They have to treat them equitably. Now I know that's kind of a big word, but what it really means is that employees need to be treated fairly.

Organizations treat people the same as a way to avoid getting sued. The theory is that if everyone is treated the same, no one is able to make a case that he/she was treated differently and, therefore, possibly discriminated against. It's the safe but ineffective way.

Once an organization starts to treat everyone the same, it fails to distinguish between good performers and bad performers. As a result, and regardless of economic conditions, good performers leave and bad performers stay.

Effective human resources practitioners focus on employee performance – improving it or addressing where it is lacking. The law, the policies, the procedures and everything else is just boring. Treating everyone the same is easier though. Insisting on addressing the poor performers and rewarding the good performers is harder and takes guts.

The real human resources professional is:

- Not afraid to draw a line in the sand.
- Not afraid to be challenged (sued) when distinctions are made among employees and one is fired and one is not.
- Not afraid to call a spade a spade.

Businesses need to be run like businesses and our employees deserve to be treated as individuals and rewarded for their efforts.

10. Don't Fire People or Discipline Poorly

Poor performers, insubordinate employees and those that act with a lack of integrity deserve to be fired. It's how it is done that matters.

When employees are disciplined or terminated in an embarrassing, demeaning or undignified manner, the reputation of the organization is harmed on many fronts – from the community perspective to the reputation of human resources.

The cautiously prudent human resources professional has been told that he/she must walk the employee to the door, lest something go awry. The former employee then asserts in his/her legal complaint that he/she was intentionally embarrassed and humiliated. This is not to suggest that employees should not be escorted by someone to the door when they are terminated. This is only to suggest that judgment be used to determine the most secure yet dignified way to terminate an employee. This may include waiting until the end of the day, after hours, agreeing to ship personal belongings home, providing cab fare for transportation home, etc. I once flew half way across the country to fire someone with a manager because it was the right thing to do considering the circumstances.

On a larger scale for group terminations, although it may be difficult, the personal touch is best. Periodically in the news there is a report of an organization that chooses efficiency over humanity and uses email or voicemail to terminate employees.

The prudent human resources professional never leaves himself/herself or the company in a potentially embarrassing situation.

ᘛᘛᘛᘛᘛᘛᘛᘛᘛ

11. Make the Rounds... Even When You are Not Going to Fire or Discipline Someone

Human resources professionals who travel to satellite facilities often earn a reputation of showing up just to terminate someone. Even those that spend most of their time in their own office develop reputations as only coming out when someone is about to go.

Human resources goes to the facility or department in order to make sure everything goes right, coordinate communication, arrange the departure of employees, etc.

What's to stop human resources from visiting when times are good? Typically the exhausted human resources professional cannot think of a good reason to go because he/she is under siege from his/her daily job.

The way to avoid the reputation of being the bearer of bad news is to visit more often when good things are happening rather than just when bad things are happening.

It's that simple.

ΛΛΛΛΛΛΛΛΛΛ

12. Help a Manager Improve Someone's Performance

The human resources professional's job is to help improve performance. Nowhere else can the human resources professional shine than in helping a manager improve his/her employees' performance. All too often managers are too close to the situation, feel a lack of confidence in managing employees, and need a sounding board when faced with a problem employee. If a manager knows you have his/her back, he/she is more likely to trust you and reach out to you in the future.

Don't just be the gate keeper and restrict your involvement in employee performance management to handling the paperwork as the offending employee goes out the door.

- Be available as a sounding board, but make sure the manager and employees know that the manager is in charge.
- Coach the manager through conversations he/she will face.
- Offer to resolve conflict within the department.

ᴎᴎᴎᴎᴎᴎᴎᴎᴎᴎ

13. Help an Employee Personally

Managers aren't the only ones that refer to the human resources department as "they." Employees not only view them in similar fashion but often perceive that the human resources department has omnipotent powers. They think rules come from human resources. Human resources is often the disseminator of policies, procedures and, unfortunately, is tagged with responsibility for their creation.

Little does the rest of the world know that human resources in many organizations has very little power. Among the management team, human resources often feels like a stepchild. It is called in after the fact to sweep up after an employee relations matter has been handled. It is called in after the fact to clean up the bodies after a mass layoff.

It is imperative that the human resources professional develop a reputation of genuinely caring for employees. The way to do this is, again, with baby steps.

Instead of sending the employee with a sick child to the benefit carrier's website, help him personally. Now I know what you are thinking: Employees are irresponsible and expect everyone to do things for them. Did it ever occur to you that this employee could be overwhelmed?

Many years ago, there was an employee in my company whose husband had been out of work for some time as the result of a workers' compensation injury. She was working as many hours as she could to make ends meet. It was near the holidays; I gave her a card in which I had tucked some cash. She tossed the card in her bag and did not open it until she had gotten home. She cried. It was twenty-five dollars. It could have been one dollar or a thousand dollars. The impact on her was that she realized that someone had been watching and someone cared.

Instead of hiding behind memos to disseminate policy, have meetings – particularly when it's bad news. If you have to implement a policy or change that no one will like, stand up and deliver the news with conviction, especially if it's the right thing to do. You will be respected immeasurably for it.

14. The Company Handbook is Not Your Handbook

Human resources is the keeper of policies, not the owner of policies. This is an area where I have particularly strong views and these have always served me well. For example, it's really OK to ask for input on policies. The more you do, the less likely you will be perceived as shoving them down the throats of your management and employees. The less you own them and the more everyone owns them, the more they are credible and perceived as fair.

Having said that, however, I also believe (and you should too) that anyone that is drafting or disseminating a policy that applies to your employees needs to involve human resources. This includes, for example, your finance department, your legal department, and your information technology department. Why?

- Human resources has a system of communicating information to employees; these other departments do not.
- Human resources is responsible for drafting and communicating policies in a manner that reflects the tone and culture of the organization.
- Human resources is the repository of all things people. Having policies developed and maintained in different areas of the company only serves to confuse people.
- The lawyers will advise that it's better that they be in one place to ensure that they are disseminated effectively and consistently.

How many times has the human resources department had to chase managers or employees down to collect completed forms, training and the like? This typically occurs for a variety of reasons:

- Your forms are not valued. In other words... "there's nothing in them for me."
- The tone and spirit is offensive, bossy or demeaning.
- They are intrusive – There must be an easier way to accomplish what you are trying to do.

~~~~~~

The human resources professional must ensure that the rules, procedures and forms they create provide value to management and employees. If they don't, the human resources department will be in a constant battle with its constituents. Rid yourself of what is unnecessary and create joint ownership of your systems. It will make life a lot easier.

~~~~~~~~~~~

15. Get Out of the Ivory Tower and Avoid Human Resources Speak

There are still employees who think that human resources resides in an ivory tower. Look at your surroundings.

- Do you have a gate keeper that greets employees before they can see you?
- Does your organization have so many employee self-help tools that the standard answer is "go to the website?"
- Do you have doors and windows that separate you from the masses?
- Do you spend the entire day in your office without seeing employees other than those you work with? That's like the technology manager not seeing computers.

When you communicate with people, speak in their business language, and when discussing human resources practices, speak in a language that they can understand. Are your job descriptions position competency profiles, role success profiles, job descriptions, or task expectation profiles?

Just as lawyers and doctors are criticized for speaking in languages no one understands, so too are human resources professionals.

ᴠᴠᴠᴠᴠᴠᴠᴠᴠ

16. Know Your Stuff

Everything you do and that comes from your department better be perfect – completely perfect. If it's not perfect, you will destroy your credibility.

If another department makes a mistake or handles something inartfully or, worse yet, completely blunders a situation, that's one thing. It is another matter entirely when human resources is sloppy. You are perceived as messing with people's lives and affecting them on a personal level.

- Don't make a mistake with their insurance enrollment.
- Don't make a mistake with their pay.
- Don't make a mistake with their performance appraisal.
- Don't give a manager a list that is incorrect.

One of the most difficult issues for me to get human resources practitioners to understand is rather simple – your files are everything. Yup. Your files. If you can't go to a file, find it complete, organized and accurate, no one will believe anything else you do or tell them. Yet, this is the area that human resources practitioners resist because file maintenance is viewed as demeaning clerical work.

∿∿

Do you think the accounts receivable and billing departments view files as unimportant? Not on your life.

In addition to perfection in administration, always remember that your foundational knowledge is only there to be
applied to performing work better, or solving problems. In
other words, at work knowledge isn't valued for knowledge
itself. It's only valued for what it enables you to do. Everyone expects that you will know and understand the latest
laws, theories, and practices. If you don't know them, get on
it. If you do, apply them with grace and style!

∿∿∿∿∿∿∿∿∿∿

17. Get Certified or Get a Degree

Many of us obtained our degrees years ago – mine
when human resources was called "Personnel."
Many others don't have formal training in either
human resources or business. Worse yet, many haven't been
in a classroom of any kind in years.

Why should you get a related degree, advanced degree or
obtain your human resources certification?

- If you have not been to school in a while, it will broad-
  en your horizons in an exhaustingly amazing way.
- Your children will respect you more.
- Your co-workers and employees will respect you more.
- Your confidence will explode!

If you have a degree, start working on another. It's good for
you.

If you are worried about whether you should obtain certification or a degree, then do both. It doesn't matter how old you are.

If it costs too much money, think about how and whether you are willing to invest in yourself or how committed you are to your career in human resources. If you still think you do not have the resources, take a course, even if it is free.

ᴎᴎᴎᴎᴎᴎᴎᴎᴎ

18. Integrity and Confidentiality – Loose Lips Sink Ships

Nothing kills a human resources career more easily than loose lips. Many employees are wary of discussing matters with the human resources department to begin with. Still, all one has to do is betray the trust of another and word will spread like wildfire throughout the organization.

What's the human resources professional to do?

- Make absolutely sure that the employee or manager you are speaking with knows your role, particularly when it comes to confidentiality. If there is any chance that you will have to disclose the contents of the conversation, make sure the other party knows of your obligations.
- Do not promise what you cannot deliver.
- Do not gossip with others.
- You can go to lunch and socialize with others but be careful of the perception that you might create.

Unfortunately, you are in human resources. People will judge you whether you like it or not.

- Be extremely careful and work every day to establish a reputation of trustworthiness and integrity.

ⁿⁿⁿⁿⁿⁿⁿⁿⁿⁿ

19. Open Your Mouth

No one will advocate for employees as well as you will. This is one of the areas in which you can shine. There are opportune times when you should open your mouth and advocate for what is right.

When employees are being treated poorly, open your mouth.

When an employee is being unnecessarily favored, open your mouth.

When a decision is being made by management that adversely affects an employee or a group of employees, step up and open your mouth.

All human resources professionals want to have the opportunity to sit at the table as a member of senior management. If you do, don't be like some of the others and shy away from advocating for employees because you think that you have to come across as a business person. It is your job to have the employees' backs. Be proud and stand up for them.

ⁿⁿⁿⁿⁿⁿⁿⁿⁿⁿ

20. You Can and Must be an Employee Advocate, but You are Still Management

Employees see you as management. The key is that you need to be prepared to strike a delicate balance between being aligned with management and being an advocate for employees.

You represent the interests of the employer but must still use your skills at conflict resolution, fight for employees who are being mistreated, and challenge management when decisions are made which will have a negative impact on employees.

The use of empathy is one of the key abilities a human resources professional can demonstrate. You do not have to agree with everyone. You just need to demonstrate that you understand their positions or situation.

∿∿∿∿∿∿∿∿∿

21. Recuse Yourself From the Yucky Stuff

Striking and maintaining a delicate balance between being the advocate for employees and a member of management can place the human resources practitioner in a slew of awkward positions. The effective human resources practitioner will know when he/she can be objective and when it is time to recuse him/herself from the situation.

As part of my practice I conduct highly sensitive workplace investigations. In most of the instances where I am retained, the human resources professional has made the right decision and recused himself/herself from conducting the investigations.

Think about whether you can be objective in the following situations?

- The CEO comes to you and asks you to embark on a salary study to determine his compensation.
- There is a major organizational turf dispute between the division you work in and another.
- The CFO of your organization has been accused of sexually harassing another employee. Should you really be doing the investigation?
- An employee is accused of sexually assaulting another on a business trip. Should you really be doing the investigation?

It is possible that you can be objective in these scenarios. However, what about the perception of your objectivity? If the weight of perception is that you could have been influenced in some way, that is enough for any prudent human resources professional to recuse himself/herself.

∿∿∿∿∿∿∿∿∿

22. Don't be Anyone's Scapegoat

Weak managers love to dump their responsibilities on others. Worse yet, sometimes these weak managers hold very senior level positions in your organization. Imagine the weak manager that is afraid or unwilling to address a performance problem with an employee. The manager then comes to you seemingly to ask for advice. Before you know it, the manager has you meeting with the employee to counsel him/her about the performance problems.

It's not your job to manage or terminate someone else's employees. It's your job to coach the manager on how to do it. Make yourself available to others, but do not take on their burdens or responsibilities.

NNNNNNNNN

23. Have Pfun

We spend more time at work than we do with our beloved family members. Work should have an element of fun and you should build fun into your work every day. Fun can build camaraderie and make employees more productive and creative. In addition, it supposedly burns more calories.

Fun can include activities at the organizational level or the departmental or individual level. Fun can be spontaneous, can increase morale, and can ultimately promote business success.

There are countless books written on how to have fun at work. Try to incorporate a little bit every day.

Oh, and one more thing: Remember to take ALL of your vacation time.

About DataMotion Publishing

We Turn Experts into Authors

DataMotion Publishing was originally established to provide books, training materials and other published periodicals to Employment Practices Advisors, Inc., a human resources consulting firm.

Now a full service publishing business, DataMotion provides publishing and related support services to subject matter experts ranging from how-to guides, training materials and practitioners resources focusing on the human resources, legal and general business areas.

Services include:

- Author and Manuscript Services
- Interior Book Design Services
- Cover Design
- Marketing and Promotion Services
- Book Website Development and SEO
- Registration Services

Our team of experts includes not only publishing and related professionals but also experienced writers and experts in the human resources, legal and business arenas.

www.datamotionpublishing.com
info@datamotionpublishing.com

∿∿∿∿∿∿∿∿∿

Also by Diane M. Pfadenhauer

Workplace Investigations: Discrimination and Harassment

The Employer's Guide to New York Employment Laws

The Employer's Guide to C.O.B.R.A. Self-Administration

New York State Employer's Legal Guide

The Employer's Guide to the Family and Medical Leave Act

Available at www.datamotionpublishing.com

∿∿∿∿∿∿∿∿∿

www.ingramcontent.com/pod-product-compliance
Lightning Source LLC
Chambersburg PA
CBHW032021190326
41520CB00007B/566